In *Thrum* Joel Allegretti, deftly and delightfully, strums his magical musical instrument, which is poetry, as he forges fresh forms of songs and stories that are inspired by strummers' strings. "Context is everything," Allegretti reminds us, and we're planted in the heart of a global ancient/modern orchestra. Prepare yourself for the revelatory performance.

Martine Bellen
Author of *Tales of Murasaki and Other Poems*,
1997 National Poetry Series selection

Joel Allegretti's latest collection of poems is as enjoyable as it is different. *Thrum* takes the reader on a journey that explores known musical instruments, such as the mandolin, dulcimer and fiddle, as well as some not-so-known instruments, such as the oud, koto and theorbo. But what makes this journey unique is that each instrument is in a sense personified as the emotive element of each instrument is brought to life. Allegretti does a wonderful job tuning every poem so that the music of each instrument is realized again and again in the words on the page. An intriguing and must read for anyone who has a sense of all that culminates in the commingling of the arts.

Raymond Hammond
Editor, *The New York Quarterly*

Also by Joel Allegretti

Father Silicon (The Poet's Press, 2006)

The Plague Psalms (The Poet's Press, 2000)

THRUM

Poems

By Joel Allegretti

POETS WEAR PRADA • HOBOKEN, NJ

THRUM

First North American Publication 2010.

Grateful acknowledgment is made to the following publications:

Illuminations	"Mandolin"
Jabberwock Review	"Autoharp"
The Laurel Review	"Appalachian Dulcimer"
Natural Bridge	"Architectural Guitar Constructions"
The New York Quarterly	"Fiddle"
Open Cut	"Psaltery"
Porcupine	"Guitar," "Oud," "Sitar"
Skidrow Penthouse	"Prepared Piano," "Prepared Piano De- and Reconstructed"

ISBN 978-0-9841844-4-6

Printed in the U.S.A.

Cover: Joel Allegretti and Roxanne Hoffman; Odd Dog font by Matthew Welch

Author Photo: Jon Paul

Contents

GUITAR

A Western stringed instrument descended from an Arabic stringed instrument. Both appear frequently in American and European concert halls. In Afghanistan both were forbidden under the Taliban, along with the faces of women.

"This machine kills fascists."[1]

The tie that binds Andres Segovia and the Clash.

A member of the family of musical instruments called chordophones, whose sound is produced by the vibration of a string. Thus, the guitar is a piano with a smaller ego.

The guitar, as we know it, originated in Spain four centuries ago. "An infanta, a Sister of Mercy, a Moor's virgin niece."[2]

Like a woman, the guitar is capable of capriciousness. In 1963 an English guitarist named Davy Graham composed a raga arrangement of the Irish tune "She Moved Through the Fair" and made no money. Several years later, an English guitarist named Jimmy Page appropriated the arrangement, changed the title to "White Summer," claimed composer credit and became wealthy. Davy Graham's devotion to the guitar relegated him to a life of poverty (the drugs also had a profound effect). Jimmy Page's devotion to the guitar enabled him to purchase a castle (the drugs had no profound effect).

MOUTH BOW

The Cree folk singer Buffy Sainte-Marie played the mouth bow on *The Tonight Show* in the early 1970s. The solitary bowstring whirring against her teeth, she trilled "Going up Cripple Creek, going in a whirl/ Going up Cripple Creek to see my girl/"[1] to the camera eye as America watched from its midnight bed.

Context is everything.

A urinal installed in a men's room is a urinal installed in a men's room. The urinal Marcel Duchamp submitted for the 1917 exhibition of the Society of Independent Artists was a spit in the eye.

Which, then, is the bolder statement: Yoko Ono emerging from a white sack before an audience of hippies or Buffy Sainte-Marie on NBC serenading Johnny Carson with a prehistoric stringed instrument?

PSALTERY

A psalmist's
Devotion rests
On each
Note
And within every
Interval.

HARP

This is where it all begins. A man mourns the loss of his beloved. She has gone from flesh to dust to mist. His voice alone fails to voice his grief. His strings become the pedestal of his bereavement: the lachrymal architecture.

Selah

The ladder for a song of degrees. The pious throat from which echo a joyful noise[1] and the annunciation of marvelous things[2]. The psaltery's kin in exultation[3].

Why do we envision angels playing the harp and not the panpipes?

Listen! Listen!
The harps, the harps,
Plucked in holy ecstasy.

Selah

Body and blood of the bard. Homer had his kithara. The Irish composer and poet O'Carolan (1670 – 1738), who shared blindness with the lord of epics, had his Celtic harp. Homer sang of Achilles and Odysseus from memory. O'Carolan played a rival's concerto note for note after one hearing.

Selah

Dear David,
Let us be a fraction of what you were in His sight.

This composition is for the chief musician upon my excellent strings.

FIDDLE

Implicated for millennia
As an emperor's diversion
While a great city collapsed in flames.

It took the fall for a lyre.

HAMMERED DULCIMER

She was borne of the Persians, who also bequeathed fine carpet weaving and death by ✞. Her given name was Santur, that is, "one hundred strings."

She is a box of chimes.

        The piano's bones laid bare.

                        A dream that Coleridge dreamed:

                                        A damsel with a dulcimer
                                        In a vision once I saw.[1]

She is the virtuoso traveler, the consummate assimilator among stringed instruments.

A guitar
                        is a guitar
                                                        is a guitar.

But she arrived in China and became Yang-chin.
She settled in Italy and was renamed Salterio.
She immigrated to Hungary to be re-christened Cimbalom.
She sailed to Ireland and was called Tiompan.
In Thailand and Cambodia her name is Khim.

OUD

For Munir Bashir and Hamza El Din

A chordophone instrument of Arabic genesis with five or six pairs of strings, often played with a plectrum made from an eagle's feather. Original name: *al'ud*, meaning "the wood." Forefather of the lute and mandolin; distant ancestor of the guitar. The Adam of plucked strings.

The heart of that archangel "who despisest an unimpassioned song."[1] Itself a seraph "whose ruby-bright throat secretes divine murmurs."[2]

The oud is a wanderer, a short-necked immigrant with the contours of a pear who migrated to the Near East, North Africa and, via Andalusia (Al-Andalus), to Europe and married into local song. The DNA of flamenco and John Dowland.

In the 10th Century an Egyptian mathematician and astronomer named Abu'l-Hasan Ali ibn Abd al-Rahman ibn Ahmad ibn Yunus al-Sadafi wrote a laudation, *Unanimities and Felicities in Praise of the Oud.*

In 1915 the Turks annihilated a million and a half Armenians. The honeyed strains of the oud flow through the musical traditions of both cultures.

SITAR

For the ancient Hindu musicians … the tones they uttered or produced were also avatars of cosmic deities or forces of Nature.
Dane Rudhyar,
The Rebirth of Hindu Music

Another way of saying "India" – just as "jazz" is a synonym for "New Orleans" (as is "sorrow"). The tremor of Vishnu's and Krishna's lotus-flecked exhalations. The Upanishads transmuted into sound waves.

The sitar is a type of lute. When we say "lute," however, we never mean "sitar." We mean "lute."

We in the West think "sitar," then think "Ravi Shankar." We think "Ravi Shankar," then think "George Harrison." We in the West tend to relate everything back to ourselves.

The instrument defies its name. Sitar (the word) translates as "three strings." Sitar (the instrument) possesses four melody strings (sometimes five) and eighteen (or so) sympathetic drone strings. Imagine if Homer had described the shape and color of the Cyclops' other eye.

PIPA

High mountain,
          flowing streams,
Snow on a sunny spring day.

☙

Floating petals
          decorating the green leaves,
Dance of the Yi tribe.

☙

The moon on high –
          Ambuscade from ten sides!
Wild geese descend on the smooth sand.

KOTO

Thirteen silken strings
Shimmer in the April breeze.
Fourteen hundred springs.

BIWA
A Haiku Essay

Of Japan's biwa
There are two things you should know:
It's a variant

Of a four-string lute
From China called the pipa,
Though not as ancient.

Now, the other thing.
In his collection *Kwaidan*
From 1904,

Lafcadio Hearn,
Who became a citizen
Of the Rising Sun

And recast himself
As Koizumi Yokumo,
Tells a ghost story

About Hōïchi
Who was a *biwa-hoshi* –
That is, a lute-priest.

You may inquire,
Why "lute-priest"? They shaved their heads
As Buddhist monks do.

The lute-priests were blind
And sang tragic histories.
In this morbid tale

Our *biwa-hoshi*,
As Lafcadio tells it,
Left demons crying.

When Orpheus sang,
The women of Thrace ripped him
Into bloody shreds

On the shores of Hell.
The lute-priest played for spirits
Who tore off his ears.

He then was known as
Mimi-nashi-Hōïchi:
Earless Hōïchi.

That was the second
Of two things re: the biwa.
Thank you for your time.

AEOLIAN HARP

Hang a sheet of paper in the wind.

Let it blow freely.

After three quarters of an hour, bring the page back inside.

Whatever has adhered to it becomes the poem.

THEORBO

Theorbo?

CELLO

Leviathan
Of the orchestral
Sea

Violin's
Magnification
Of itself

Cellar
Of the string section's
Architecture

☙

In his closing decade
Pablo Casals
Played it

For world harmony
He bowed
It lowed:

Dona
Nobis
Pacem[1]

His weapon
Of mass
Redemption

MANDOLIN

You are the runt of the lute's litter, the parasitic twin excised from its half-pear belly. Sideshow dwarf to the guitar's trapeze artist and bass fiddle's strong man. You ring with tarantellas and bluegrass. You *plink, plink, plink* for revelers sweating spider poison and parry with the banjo at Saturday night clog dances. You are *limoncello* and moonshine, the Apennines and Appalachians, Vivaldi's *Concerto in G Major* and Bill Monroe's *Blue Moon of Kentucky.*

BANJO

Sired by Africans,
In the popular mind
An emblem of the white rural South,
It crossed the color barrier before its creators.

Great-great-great grandchild of *Mbanza*,
Who knew the clatter of manacles
And the stench of slave ships.

String and drum centaur.

The guitar was fathered
By European conquerors.
An index of illustrious
Afro-American
Guitar players
Reads like
A royal bloodline of
Vernacular music:

Son House,
Charlie Patton,
Robert Johnson,
Memphis Minnie,
Leadbelly,
Skip James,
Etc.

An index of illustrious
Afro-American
Banjo players
Reads thus:

,
,
,
,
,
,

Etc.

APPALACHIAN DULCIMER

Of truth William James wrote, "Truth is essentially a relation between two things, an idea, on the one hand, and a reality outside of the idea, on the other. This relation, like all relations, has its *fundamentum*, namely, the matrix of experiential circumstance, psychological, as well as physical, in which the correlated terms are found embedded."

The truth is the Appalachian dulcimer is not a true dulcimer. It is a fretted zither.

AUTOHARP®

Little yellow-headed girl in the red dress,
Sweet melancholy attic child,
Don't you weep because the preacher
Bat-songed his way into your secret cupboard.
There is no simple road to Paradise.
It's the brambles that make the difference.
No, don't you weep, my wildwood flower.
Mama will buy you new shoes.
Crow Jane will oath on the Good Book
That you're a proper girl. And the stars,
Oh, they know what makes the church bells ring.
Listen! Hear that? Out on the back steps –
Poor Howard's thumb-dancing
On his autoharp, singing all about you:
"Oh, the cuckoo, she's a pretty bird,
She warbles as she flies."[1]

® Autoharp is a registered trademark of Oscar Schmidt, a division of U.S. Music Corp. Is it the Kleenex® and Xerox® of musical instruments?

® Kleenex is a registered trademark of Kimberly-Clark Corporation.

® Xerox is a registered trademark of Xerox Corporation.

BASS

It was suddenly me.
It wasn't the bass anymore.
Charles Mingus

MINGUS MINGUS MINGUS MINGUS
MINGUS MINGUS MINGUS MINGUS
MINGUS MINGUS MINGUS MINGUS
MINGUS MINGUS MINGUS MINGUS
MINGUS MINGUS MINGUS MINGUS
MINGUS MINGUS MINGUS MINGUS
MINGUS MINGUS MINGUS MINGUS
MINGUS MINGUS MINGUS MINGUS
MINGUS MINGUS MINGUS MINGUS
MINGUS MINGUS MINGUS MINGUS
MINGUS MINGUS MINGUS MINGUS
MINGUS MINGUS MINGUS MINGUS
MINGUS MINGUS MINGUS MINGUS
MINGUS MINGUS MINGUS MINGUS
MINGUS MINGUS MINGUS MINGUS
MINGUS MINGUS MINGUS MINGUS
MINGUS MINGUS MINGUS MINGUS
MINGUS MINGUS MINGUS MINGUS
MINGUS MINGUS MINGUS MINGUS
MINGUS MINGUS MINGUS MINGUS
MINGUS MINGUS MINGUS MINGUS
MINGUS MINGUS MINGUS MINGUS
MINGUS MINGUS MINGUS MINGUS
MINGUS MINGUS MINGUS MINGUS
MINGUS MINGUS MINGUS MINGUS
MINGUS MINGUS MINGUS MINGUS
MINGUS MINGUS MINGUS MINGUS
MINGUS MINGUS MINGUS MINGUS
MINGUS MINGUS MINGUS MINGUS
MINGUS MINGUS MINGUS MINGUS
MINGUS MINGUS MINGUS MINGUS

PREPARED PIANO

In $E = MC^2$ we see embedded the name of Albert Einstein. In every angle of the geodesic dome are Buckminster Fuller's initials. The strings of the prepared piano vibrate the letters J-O-H-N-C-A-G-E.

John Cage devised the instrument in the late 1930s, when he was commissioned to compose music for a dance piece. He originally wrote for percussion instruments, but the performance area was too small to accommodate an ensemble. The room had a piano, though, on which he pondered the possibilities.

The ancients conceived the gryphon, a creature part-lion and part-eagle, but neither lion nor eagle. Cage fitted the strings of the piano with bolts, rubber stops and screws to replicate percussion sounds, creating an instrument that was neither percussion nor wholly piano.

The absence of available space gave the prepared piano its place in the world.

PREPARED PIANO DE- AND RECONSTRUCTED

The strings of the prepared piano pondered the possibilities. The strings of the piano gave the prepared instrument neither lion nor eagle, but space. The dome wrote for percussion piano. We see the piano gryphon embedded in every angle of the absence of Buckminster Fuller's initials.

The ancients conceived an ensemble with bolts, rubber stops and screws.

Commissioned to compose, the room had the letters J-O-H-N-C-A-G-E to replicate available percussion sounds.

He, John Cage, devised the name of Albert Einstein in the late 1930s when he was neither percussion nor wholly the world. In $E=MC^2$ vibrates a piano, a creature part-lion and part-performance area, creating an instrument that was too small to accommodate music for a geodesic dance piece.

ARCHITECTURAL GUITAR CONSTRUCTIONS

For John Fahey and Davy Graham

1st String/High E

Of the six strings, this one is nearest heaven, tempered by the spit of angels. Its harmonics shimmer millimeters below the firmament and tickle the chin of the moon. It threads through the Cloud of Unknowing, uttering one of God's names with each reverberation. In more earthly moods, it will mimic the songs of the nightingale, dove and scarlet tanager. The planets themselves bore this string, but in all humility it prefers to believe it is descended from bells and resides in a Gothic tower.

2nd String/B

The waspstring.

The nettlestring.

The serpentstring.

The hummingstring.

Obedient drone to E.

Tabernacle of middle C.

3rd String/G

G has nothing to do with strippers or fan dancers.

G is the border string, lying on the cusp of treble and bass, negotiating a common purpose, i.e., the wholeness of sound.

G is a quenching river: Those on either bank may draw sustenance from its waters.

G's loyalties, however, ultimately rest with its two higher-pitched brethren. After all, the treble clef is better known as G clef. When G and the three lower strings play simultaneously, their confluence lays a cellar of discord. But when G, B and High E are struck at once, they erect a gable of harmony: the E minor chord. It is the only chord that can be played on open strings. Why a minor chord? What reason has the guitar to be so melancholy?

4th String/D

The Sir Richard Burton
and Sir Walter Raleigh string.

Globetrotter.

Adventurer.

Vessel of cultures.

What are the similarities between an Irish air and an Indian raga?
The D string knows.

This string is an ashram on the outskirts of Bombay.

A shotgun shack on the Mississippi Delta.

A vendor's stall in a Marrakech souk.

A general store in Kentucky.

A wine bar in London.

Chameleon.

Proteus.

The Zelig string.

5th String/A

A is the creator string. The other five evolved out of its 440 emanations.

The Gnostics hypothesized the Pleroma, a prototype deity who emanated another deity who emanated another who emanated another and so on until the 365th and final emanation: God, who made this world. So removed is God from the Pleroma that He is a pale, attenuated resolution of His parent. Therefore, a degenerated deity created a degenerate world.

A's emanations have no such imperfections.

6th String/Low E

Earthy yin to High E's ethereal yang.

The string geographically closest to the player's heart.

Notes

"Guitar"

[1] Slogan on Woody Guthrie's guitar.
[2] Allegretti, Joel. From the "Manitas de Plata" section of "Anthology of Hands." *The Plague Psalms* (The Poet's Press, 2000).

"Mouth Blow"

[1] Trad. "Cripple Creek."

"Harp"

[1] Psalms 66 and 100.
[2] Psalm 98.
[3] Psalm 150.

"Oud"

[1] Poe, Edgar Allan. "Israfel."
[2] Allegretti, Joel. "Al'Ud." *The Plague Psalms* (The Poet's Press, 2000).

"Hammered Ducimer"

[1] Coleridge, Samuel Taylor. "Kubla Khan."

"Pipa"

The poem is made up of the seven track titles on *Floating Petals … Wild Geese … the Moon on High: Music of the Chinese Pipa* by Lui Pui-yuen, Nonesuch Records, 1980.

"Cello"

[1] Grant Us Peace.

"Autoharp"

[1] Trad. "The Cuckoo."

Acknowledgments

The phrase "architectural guitar constructions" first appeared in a *New York Times* music review by Jon Pareles.

I extend my deepest thanks to Martine Bellen, who suggested a series on musical instruments after my completion of "Guitar" and "Oud."

About the Author

Joel Allegretti is the author of *The Plague Psalms*, which appeared in 2000 and is now in its third edition, and *Father Silicon*, selected by *The Kansas City Star* as one of 100 Noteworthy Books of 2006.

Allegretti's work has appeared in many national journals, including *The New York Quarterly*, *Margie*, *The Laurel Review*, *Art/Life Limited Editions*, *Rattapallax*, *Slipstream*, *Confrontation*, and *Xcp Cross-Cultural Poetics*. He is represented in the anthology *Chance of a Ghost* (Helicon Nine Editions, 2005), and his poem in that collection received an Honorable Mention in the 2006 edition of *The Year's Best Fantasy and Horror*, published by St. Martin's Press.

In April 2009, Kean University in New Jersey presented the world premiere of a song cycle based on Allegretti's poetry, "A Cycle by the Sea" by Frank Ezra Levy, who served several decades as cellist with the Radio City Music Hall Orchestra and whose symphonic work is available in the American Classics series on Naxos.

Allegretti is a graduate of New York University and lives in Northern New Jersey. His website is www.joelallegretti.com.

www.ingramcontent.com/pod-product-compliance
Lightning Source LLC
LaVergne TN
LVHW010549100826
845148LV00013B/2665

9780984184446